Claymation Sensation

SPORTS CLAYMATION

Emily Reid

Published in 2017 by **Windmill Books**,
an Imprint of Rosen Publishing
29 East 21st Street, New York, NY 10010

Produced for Rosen by BlueAppleWorks Inc.

Creative Director: Melissa McClellan
Managing Editor for BlueAppleWorks: Melissa McClellan
Design: T.J. Choleva
Editor: Kelly Spence
Puppet Artisans: Janet Kompare-Fritz (p. 16, 18, 22); Jane Yates (p.12, 14, 20)

Picture credits: Plasticine letters:Vitaly Korovin/Shutterstock; title page, TOC, Austen Photography; p. 4 Sony Pictures Releasing/Photofest; p.5 Janet Kompare-Fritz; ; p. 6 left to right and top to bottom: ukrfidget/Shutterstock; Andrey Eremin/Shutterstock; exopixel /Shutterstock; Lukas Gojda/Shutterstock; koosen/Shutterstock; Irina Nartova/Shutterstock; STILLFX/Shutterstock; Picsfive/Shutterstock; Darryl Brooks/Shutterstock; Winai Tepsuttinun/Shutterstock; Yulia elf_inc Tropina/Shutterstock; Austen Photography; All For You /Shutterstock; Radu Bercan /Shutterstock; Austen Photography; p. 7 left to right and top to bottom: Ilike/Shutterstock; Tarzhanova/Shutterstock; Austen Photography; kamomeen /Shutterstock; Lesha/Shutterstock; ikurdyumov/Shutterstock; Austen Photography; Ilike/Shutterstock; p-8 to 27 Austen Photography; p. 28 left Valentina Razumova/Shutterstock; p. 29 upper left Warongdech/Shutterstock;p. 29 top right Anneka/Shutterstock; p. 29 right taelove7/Shutterstock; p. 30, 31 Austen Photography; p. 31 right Samuel Borges Photography/Shutterstock

Cataloging-in-Publication Data
Names: Reid, Emily.
Title: Sports claymation / Emily Reid.
Description: New York : Windmill Books, 2017. | Series: Claymation sensation | Includes index.
Identifiers: ISBN 9781499481044 (pbk.) | ISBN 9781499481068 (library bound) | ISBN 9781499481051 (6 pack)
Subjects: LCSH: Animation (Cinematography)--Juvenile literature. | Sculpture--Technique--Juvenile literature. | Sports in art--Juvenile literature.
Classification: LCC TR897.5 R45 2017 | DDC 777'.7--dc23

Manufactured in the United States of America
CPSIA Compliance Information: Batch #BS16PK: For Further Information contact Rosen Publishing, New York, New York at 1 800 237 9932

Contents

What Is Claymation?

Get ready to win big with your very own sports Claymation! Claymation, also known as clay **animation**, combines **stop-motion** animation with characters or puppets made out of modeling clay to create movies or short videos.

Stop-motion animation creates the illusion of movement when a series of still images, called **frames**, are quickly played in sequence. Each frame shows a slight change in position from the previous frame. Clay characters are easy to move and reposition to show these actions in small steps. The smaller the movements, the smoother the sequence appears. It takes several frames to make a Claymation movie. Animations can be created using many devices, including a traditional camera, smartphone, or tablet.

The Pirates! Band of Misfits *is a 3-D Claymation movie that was released in 2012. All of the film's puppets were handmade. For each frame, animators had to carefully position each character on the set.*

Claymation Tip

There are lots of apps you can use to create your Claymation movie. These apps let you shoot and edit your movie using one device. Make sure to ask permission before you download any apps to your smartphone, tablet, or computer.

All types of filmmaking, including Claymation, tell a story. To start, brainstorm an idea for your sports adventure. Think of a beginning, middle, and end. Write a short summary of the story. How many characters do you need to tell your story? What kind of background and props will you use?

When you make a Claymation movie, it is important to map out the character's movements before you start shooting. A **storyboard** is a series of drawings that show each step of the story. Use a storyboard to figure out what actions are needed, and in what order, to tell your story from start to finish. Sketch out each scene and label it with the scene number. After the storyboard is ready, it's time to create your puppets.

A storyboard showing six frames.

Scene 1

Scene 2

Scene 3

Scene 4

Scene 5

Scene 6

Materials and Techniques

Claymation puppets are created with nondrying, oil-based clay. Plasticine is a popular brand, although any nondrying modeling clay will do. This type of clay is moldable enough to create a character, flexible enough to allow that character to move in many ways, and dense enough to hold its shape when combined with a wire **armature**.

Materials That You Will Need

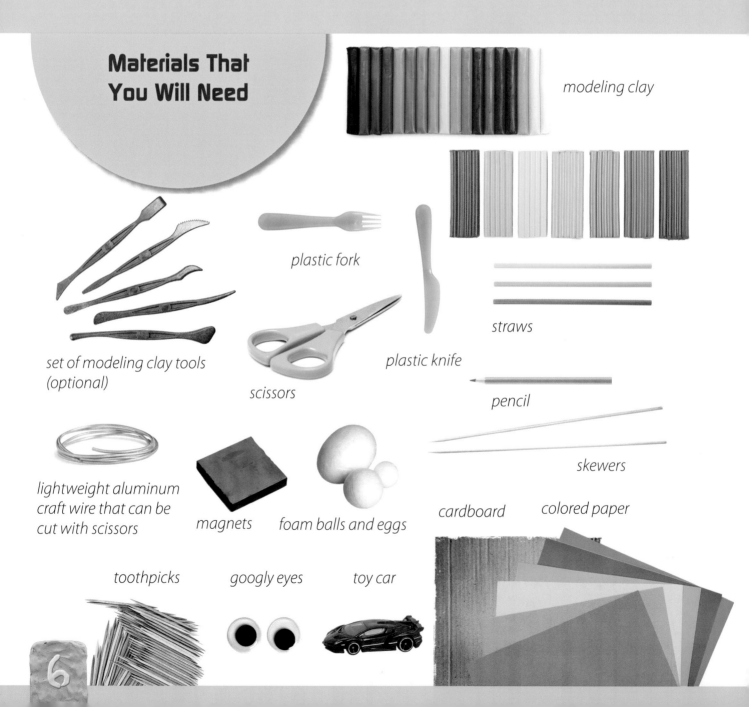

modeling clay

set of modeling clay tools (optional)

plastic fork

scissors

plastic knife

straws

pencil

skewers

lightweight aluminum craft wire that can be cut with scissors

magnets

foam balls and eggs

cardboard

colored paper

toothpicks

googly eyes

toy car

Working with Clay

Modeling clay is oily and can be messy to work with. Prepare a work area. A piece of cardboard or foam board is great to work on. Wash your hands well when you finish working, as they will be oily, too.

Basic Shapes

All of these shapes can be made big or small or thin or thick, depending on the amount of clay used and the pressure applied. Use your fingers to squish, smooth, pinch, flatten, and poke the clay into whatever shape you want.

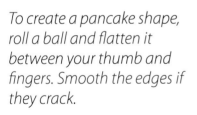

To form a ball, move your hands in a circle while pressing the clay lightly between them.

To create a pancake shape, roll a ball and flatten it between your thumb and fingers. Smooth the edges if they crack.

To make a snake shape, roll the clay on a flat surface with your fingers. Roll a pencil over the snake to flatten it and make a ribbon.

To form a teardrop, pinch and roll one end of a ball into a point.

To create a cylinder, roll a large piece of clay in your hand, then roll it on a flat surface to smooth. Press each end into the table to flatten it.

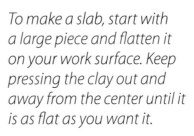

To make a slab, start with a large piece and flatten it on your work surface. Keep pressing the clay out and away from the center until it is as flat as you want it.

Modeling Tips

- Always start by kneading the clay in your hands to warm it up and soften it.

- You can mix different colors together to create new colors. Just squish the clay in your hands until it is blended completely or leave it partially blended to create a marble effect.

- Make your puppets about the same size as an action figure, between 4 and 6 inches (10 and 15 cm) tall. They should be big enough to move around but not so big they fall over.

Body Parts and Armatures

Puppets can be made in many ways. The simple ones require only modeling clay and some patience. If you decide to create more complicated puppets, you will need additional elements to give the puppets structure and support, such as wire armatures and foam shapes. It is a good idea to keep anything that is on top of the puppet light so it does not droop during animation. Using a lightweight foam ball should do the trick.

1 Get different size foam shapes from a local craft or dollar store.

2 Carefully cover the foam with a thin layer of clay.

3 Smooth any bumps with your fingers until you have an even surface.

4 Attach the puppet's legs and arms to the finished head. Make sure that your puppet can stand up on its own. You are ready to roll!

Claymation Tip

Use foam shapes to create bulky body parts. This makes your puppets lighter and reduces the amount of clay that you will need to create puppets.

Stability

Make sure your character has a big enough base or feet to support its weight. If necessary, you can stabilize it with putty or put pushpins through the puppet's feet to hold it in place.

Armatures

Armatures function as a skeleton that holds the puppet parts together and allows for them to move easily. Wire-based armatures are made using strands of lightweight wire. Whenever useful, you can combine an armature with foam pieces to create a base for your puppet. Make sure you don't make the clay too thick around the armature, or your puppet will be difficult to move.

Be creative with the details. Try new things. Use carving tools on some puppets. Have fun with it!

To make an armature for a figure, start with a long piece of wire. Fold it in half. Twist the wire to form a loop at the top.

Take one piece of the wire and bend it to form one of the figure's arms. You can make it whatever length you choose. At the end of the arm, loop the wire and twist it back on itself. Repeat this step on the opposite side using the other length of wire.

Twist both wires together to form the body.

Make the legs and feet following the same steps used for the arms. If you have extra wire left, cut it off or wind it around the body.

Use a foam ball for the head to make the puppet lighter.

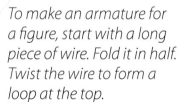

9

Facial Expressions and Body Language

A puppet's facial features include its eyes, nose, mouth, and eyebrows. The way these features are positioned can make your puppet look shocked or scared, happy or sad. Simply adding eyebrows can completely change the look on your puppet's face. Try some of these techniques to add expression to your Claymation characters.

Googly Eyes

Googly eyes can be pressed directly onto the puppet's face.

Clay Eyes

Make clay eyes by rolling two small white balls. Then flatten two smaller black balls onto the white ones for pupils.

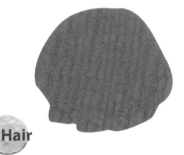

Hair

To make hair, roll a small, thin slab. Add texture with the end of a straw or a modeling tool.

Eyebrows

For eyebrows, use brown or black clay to roll two thin snakes. Place one over each eye. Arch the eyebrows to show surprise. Point them downward to create an angry expression.

Teeth

For teeth, cut rectangles out of a thin white slab.

Loops

Loops can be wrapped around a puppet's neck, arms, or legs. To make a loop, roll a skinny snake. Wrap it around the chosen body part. Join the ends together by gently pressing down where they overlap.

10

Mouth Shapes

Using certain mouth shapes is a great way to show how your character is feeling. Use thin snakes to form lips that you can easily position. You can change the puppet's expression between frames as needed.

Gloomy Expression
Make your puppet look sad by having its mouth closed and pointed downward.

Shocked Expression
Create a shocked expression by forming an O shape.

Happy Expression
Show that your puppet is happy by curving its mouth into a big smile.

Gross Expression
Show that your puppet is grossed out with a slightly open, but narrow and straight mouth shape.

Use body language to accompany your puppet's facial expressions. Try pairing some of these body positions with the above facial expressions in your Claymation movie.

Gloomy Body Language

To show gloom, place the puppet's arms down alongside its body.

Shocked Body Language

To show shock, position the puppet's arms down and away from its body.

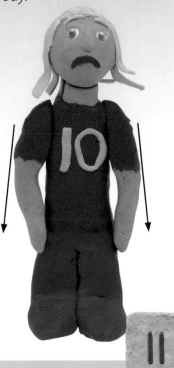

Happy Body Language
To show joy, raise the puppet's arms up and away from its body.

Soccer Player Puppet

Soccer is the most popular sport in the world. Outside of North America it is known as football. The game is played on a field with a net at each end. Players run up and down the field, trying to score in the other team's net. Only the goalie is allowed to touch the ball, so soccer involves a lot of fancy footwork.

1 *Roll two thick blue cylinders for the legs. Bend the bottom of each leg forward to make a flat foot.*

2 *For the body, form a red rectangle. Round one end to make shoulders. Press the body onto the legs and smooth the seams.*

3 *Use a foam ball for the puppet's head. Cover the foam with a thin layer of clay. Roll a short cylinder for the neck. Push a short piece of wire through the neck and head. Attach it to the body as shown.*

4 *For sleeves, roll two short red cylinders. To make arms, use beige clay to roll two longer cylinders. Firmly press each sleeve onto an arm.*

5 Push a piece of wire or toothpick through the top of the puppet's body. Attach an arm to each end.

6 Press two googly eyes onto the face. Use clay to make a nose, eyebrows, and mouth.

7 Roll a ribbon of yellow clay. Use scissors to cut the ribbon into shorter pieces. Press each ribbon onto the top of the puppet's head. Curl the ends.

8 Add a number to the front of the jersey using ribbons of orange clay.

Claymation Tip

It's game time! In your animation, you can make the puppet kick the ball down the field to score a goal. You can also make two soccer players and show them passing the ball back and forth.

13

Karate Master Puppet

Karate is an ancient Japanese martial art. The word "karate" means "open hand." This disciplined sport focuses on self-defense. It involves striking an opponent with kicks, jabs, and punches. Different colored belts show a person's level of skill. A black belt is worn by a karate master.

1 *For the feet, make two small, flat ovals. Roll two cylinders for the puppet's legs. Use the plastic knife to cut one end of each leg on a diagonal. Gently press each leg onto a foot.*

2 *For the body, roll a thick oval. Attach the legs to the bottom of the body. Use your fingers to smooth the seams.*

3 *For the arms, roll two long brown cylinders. Squeeze each cylinder a bit at one end to create wrists. Press an arm onto each side of the body. Smooth out the seams.*

4 *For the head, use a foam ball covered with clay. Roll a small cylinder for the neck. Press the head onto the neck and the neck onto the body.*

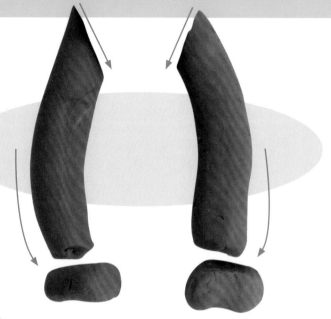

5 Roll a thin slab of white clay. Wrap it around the puppet's waist. Use scissors to cut a slit down the center of the front and back. To make pants, pinch the edges together around each leg.

6 To make sleeves, wrap a thin slab of white clay around each arm. Next, drape a slab of white clay over each shoulder. Press the slabs together and smooth the seams.

7 Use clay to add hair, eyes, nose, eyebrows, and ears to the head.

8 Roll a long thin ribbon of black clay. Wrap it around the puppet's waist. Fold each end back on itself to create a knot. Use a modeling tool to add fingers and toes to the puppet's hands and feet.

Claymation Tip

During animation, you can move the puppet's arms and legs to show kicks and jabs. You can even have your karate master break a board in half. Use your imagination. Smooth the clay if it creases between movements.

15

Hockey Player Puppet

Hockey is a fast-paced game that is popular across North America. The first hockey game was played in Montreal, Canada, during the 1800s. During a game, players zoom up and down the ice chasing the puck. There are six players on each side. They use skill and speed to try to shoot the puck past the goalie and into the net.

1 *For skate blades, press out two thin slabs. Place two toothpicks on each slab. Wrap the clay around the sticks. Trim off any extra clay. Use your fingers to smooth the seams.*

2 *Make the skate boot by pressing together a small cylinder and a large cylinder. Use the scissors to cut two short sticks. Wrap clay around the middle of each stick. Push the top of each stick into the skate and the bottom into the blade. Repeat this step for the second skate.*

3 *For legs, roll two white and two blue cylinders. Stack a blue cylinder on a white one. Push a toothpick through the cylinders to join the leg and skate together.*

4 *For the puppet's body, stick a toothpick into the top of a foam egg. Spread a thin layer of brown clay around the base of the stick and over the top of the egg. Cover the rest of the body with red clay. For the bottom of the jersey, use red and blue clay to roll two snakes. Press the snakes together and smooth them around the bottom of the egg. Leave the bottom edge loose.*

5 *To make a collar, combine a white ribbon and a red snake. Wrap the collar around the puppet's neck.*

6 Press the body onto the legs. Roll two thick red cylinders for arms. Use a toothpick to attach an arm to each side of the puppet's body.

7 Use brown clay to roll two small ovals. Cover most of the ball with a thin layer of red clay. Leave some brown clay for the wrist. Add a red thumb. Wrap a flat blue and white ribbon around the bottom of the glove. Repeat this step to make a second glove. Stick a toothpick into each glove and attach one to each arm.

8 For the head, cover a small foam ball with clay. Add eyes, a nose, ears, and teeth. Use a toothpick to attach the head to the neck.

9 Make a helmet by covering the head with a thin red slab. Use a gray ribbon for a chin strap. Add a blue stripe along the top of the helmet.

 10 Decorate the uniform with blue snakes and red ribbons. Make a team logo for the front of the jersey.

Claymation Tip

When animating your puppet, you can move its arms or legs. You can show your player celebrating after scoring a goal. (See page 24 for how to make a hockey stick and puck.)

17

Skateboarder Puppet

Skateboarding is an exciting extreme sport. Skateboarders use one foot to push the board along. They "carve" by leaning and pressing on the board to steer. Skilled skateboarders grind down rails and perform high-flying jumps like 360-degree turns. The sport can be dangerous, so skateboarders wear helmets and pads to prevent injuries.

1

To make this skateboarder, twist a long piece of wire into an armature as shown on page 9.

2

Use a foam ball for the head. Use a plastic knife to cut a slit in the foam. Press the foam onto the top loop of the armature.

3

Soften a ball of beige or brown clay. Completely cover the armature. Leave the feet bare. Add extra clay to make the body fuller. Pinch out a hand at the end of each arm.

4

To make shoes, roll two oval shapes. Press one shoe onto each of the wire feet. Fold the clay to cover the wire.

5

Cover the top of each shoe with a thin layer of blue clay. Cut a black ribbon into small pieces. Press the pieces onto each shoe in a crisscross pattern to make laces.

6 Make sleeves by covering the skater's arms with two thin white slabs. For the shirt collar, loop a white ribbon around the neck. Cover the arms with two short pieces of thin red clay to make T-shirt sleeves. Add a thin layer of red clay to build the rest of the shirt. Cover the legs with black clay. Use your fingers to smooth the seams.

7 Press two googly eyes onto the face. Add a nose. Use a modeling tool to carve a mouth. For hair, press thin brown snakes onto the puppet's head.

8 Make a helmet for your skateboarder. Press out a thin black slab and place it over the head. Use a ribbon of gray clay for a chin strap. Place the ribbon under the puppet's chin and attach the strap to each side of the helmet. Use white squares to make elbow and knee pads. Wrap two ribbons around each elbow and knee to hold the pads on.

Claymation Tip

Your skateboarder can roll across the set and perform different tricks. You can also position the puppet's arms. (See page 25 for instructions to make the skateboard.)

Figure Skater Puppet

Figure skating has been an Olympic sport since 1908. In this popular event, skaters jump and spin across the ice in a routine set to music. Some skaters perform alone while others work in pairs. Judges score a skater's performance based on their technique and style.

1 *To make this puppet, twist a long piece of wire into an armature as shown on page 9. Instead of making two legs, just continue twisting the wire together. Form a loop at the bottom. Bend the arms up into a circle above the puppet's body.*

2 *Use a foam ball for the head. Use a plastic knife to cut a slit in the foam. Press the foam onto the top loop of the armature. Soften a ball of beige or brown clay. Use the clay to cover the head, neck, and shoulders.*

3 *Cover the arms with clay. Use pink clay to add a thick layer of clay to the body. Pinch and smooth the clay until you are happy with the skater's shape. Use two ribbons of pink clay to add shoulder straps to the leotard.*

4 *Make a base for the puppet. Place the bottom loop into an old lid. Cover it with white clay.*

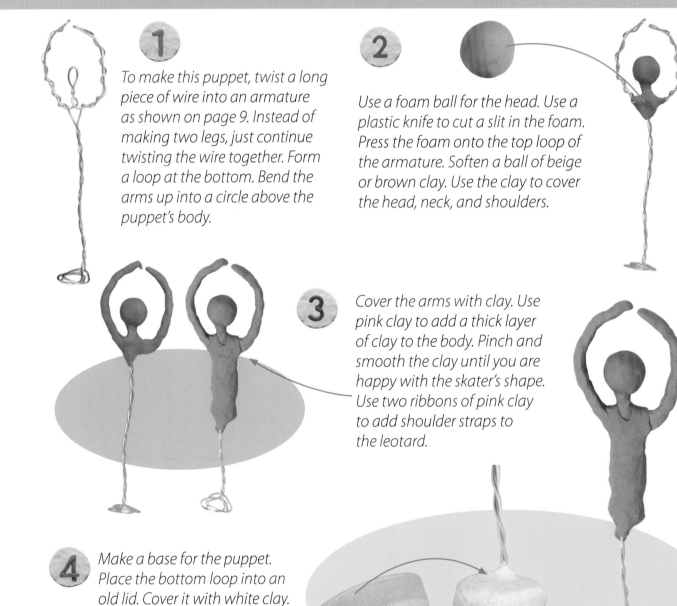

5 To make legs, roll two beige cylinders. Pinch the ends into rounded points. Roll two thin white ribbons. Wrap a ribbon around the end of each leg.

6 Make ice skates by rolling two white ovals. For blades, cover a short toothpick with gray clay. Press a blade onto the bottom of each skate. Use a toothpick to join a skate to each leg.

7 Press the legs under the body. Wrap each leg around the armature as shown. Cross the skater's ankles together at the front. Make sure the wire is completely covered.

8 Roll a thin slab for hair. Attach some snakes for a ponytail. Wrap a pink loop around the ponytail. Press it onto the back of the puppet's head. Add eyebrows, eyes, a nose, and a mouth. (See pages 10 and 11.)

9 To make a skirt, roll a thin pink ribbon. Wrap the ribbon around the skater's waist. Next, roll a thin pink pancake. Use the plastic knife to cut a circle in the middle and a slit through one side. Wrap the pancake around the body, just below the waist. Blend the two pieces together. Use your fingers to arrange the skirt so it looks like it is floating while the skater twirls.

Claymation Tip

Create an animation of your skater doing a beautiful spin. Slowly rotate the puppet, taking photos in tiny increments, until you have completed a full 360-degree turn.

21

Skier Puppet

Skiing is a popular winter sport. In downhill skiing, people fly down snow-covered hills on two long skis. Their feet are strapped into boots that click into bindings on each ski. Some skiers use poles to steer. Skilled skiers can do fancy flips and turns after going off a jump.

This puppet is flat on one side. During animation, only one side will be used.

1 *For the ski boot, roll an oval and a short cylinder. Press them together and smooth the seam. Make a pink cylinder for the bottom half of the leg. Use a toothpick to attach the boot to the leg.*

2 *Make a pink oval for the upper half of the leg. Insert a toothpick to attach it to the lower leg on an angle. The skier's knees should appear bent as shown.*

3 *Roll a short, wide oval for the body. Pinch one end to make the waist. Use a toothpick to attach the leg to the body.*

4 *Roll two pink cylinders. Bend each cylinder into a narrow V shape. Arrange one elbow so it is below the other arm as shown. Press the arms together. Use a toothpick to attach the arms to the body.*

5 *Make a yellow mitten. Push a short toothpick into the mitten, then attach it to the front arm.*

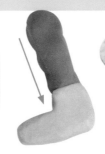

6 For the head, use the plastic knife to carefully cut a foam ball in half. Cover the rounded side with beige clay. Add extra clay to make a nose. Place a thin brown pancake on top of the head for hair.

7 Use a modeling tool to carve a mouth. Make an eye and press it onto the skier's face. Mold one ear and press it onto the side of the head. For a helmet, make a flat pink half circle and press it onto the top of the head. Add a loop around the ear.

8 For goggles, loop a thin yellow snake around the eye. Wrap the end of the snake around the skier's head. For hair, twist together several skinny brown snakes. Press them onto the back of the head, under the helmet.

9 Decorate the helmet and ski suit with thin yellow snakes. Decorate the boots with pink and gray clay. (See page 25 for directions on how to make skis and ski poles.)

Claymation Tip

Use two magnets to animate your skier. Press one magnet into the back of the puppet. When you're ready to start shooting, place the skier on the front of the set. Match the other magnet on the other side. You can now show the skier zooming down a snowy slope.

The Props

Props are used in the creation of the movie. They decorate the set. Props add visual interest to the movie. Sometimes the puppets interact with them. Brainstorm ideas about what you might see at a sporting event.

1. *Make a soccer ball. Use white clay to roll a ball or to cover a small foam ball. Roll out a thin slab of black clay. Use the plastic knife to cut out six five-sided shapes. Press each shape onto the ball.*

2. *To make a hockey puck, use black clay to roll a fat cylinder. Use the knife to cut a thick slice off. Use a yellow ribbon to decorate the top of the puck.*

3. *Make a stick for your hockey player. Cut a stick shape out of cardboard, then cover it with brown clay. Wrap black clay around the blade to represent tape. Coil blue and black snakes around the end. Add your initials.*

4. *Build a net. Bend craft wire to form a frame as shown. Cover the wire with red clay. Hang a piece of white netting on the frame.*

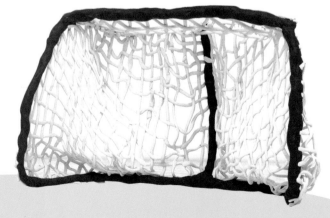

5 To make skis, cut out two pieces of cardboard in the shape of skis. Cover the cardboard in yellow clay. Add three small pieces of clay to one ski. Press the other ski onto the clay so it slightly overlaps.

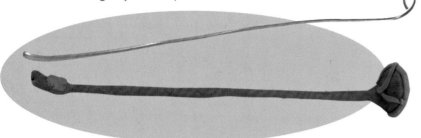

6 For ski poles, cut two pieces of wire. Make a small loop at one end of each pole. Cover the wire with gray clay. Add extra clay to the end with the loop. Decorate the poles with pink snakes.

7 Make a skateboard. Cover an old toy car (or buy one from a dollar store) with clay. Leave the wheels uncovered and make sure they can still spin. Cut a skateboard out of cardboard and cover it with clay. Press it firmly onto the top of the car. Add four wheels.

8 Make a skating rink by rolling white clay into an oval or rectangular shape.

You can also use a dry-erase board or piece of white paper to make a skating rink.

The Set

The set is where you will film your movie. It is the landscape in which your story will come to life. A set can be as simple as a piece of paper taped to the wall or more complex. The set needs to be large enough for your puppets to be able to move around.

Basic Set

The most basic set is a single piece of paper or poster board. Tape one end of the paper to the wall. Pull the paper and tape the other end to the table. Leave a bit of a curve in the paper.

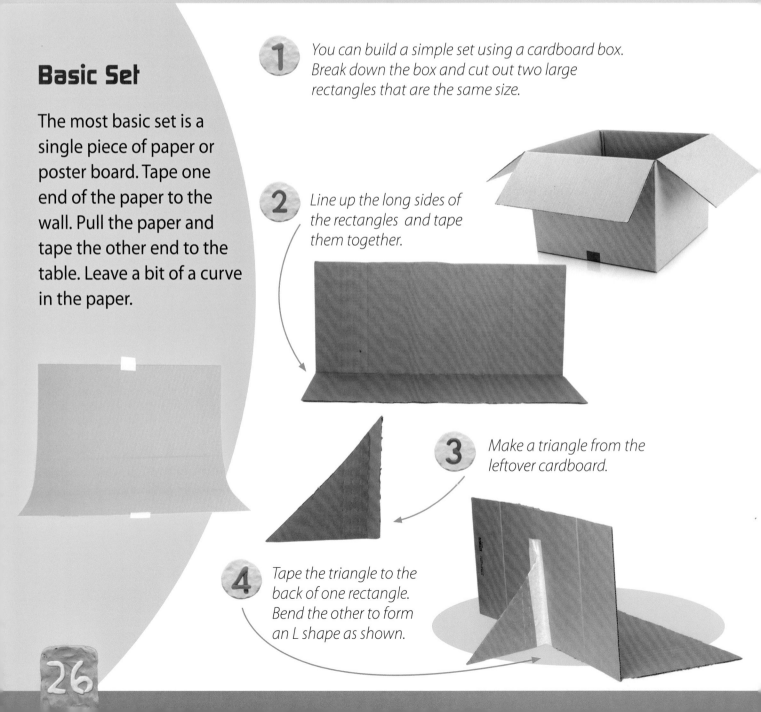

1 *You can build a simple set using a cardboard box. Break down the box and cut out two large rectangles that are the same size.*

2 *Line up the long sides of the rectangles and tape them together.*

3 *Make a triangle from the leftover cardboard.*

4 *Tape the triangle to the back of one rectangle. Bend the other to form an L shape as shown.*

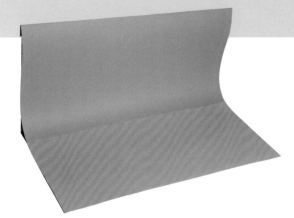

 Fold a piece of colored paper over the top of the box. Use clear or double-sided tape to secure each end of the paper to the front and back of the set.

 Tear a piece of green paper to represent a grassy field. Line it up with the sides of the box and tape in place.

 Arrange your props. Before you start shooting, secure the set to the surface you are working on with tape.

Try This!

Draw a ski slope on white poster board for your skier puppet. Add snowy mountains and pine trees to the background. Tape the poster board to the cardboard set.

Create a city background for your Claymation. Cut rectangles from construction paper to create skyscrapers rising in the distance. Add a path cut from a piece of thick cardboard.

Alternative Set

You can paint a background directly on the cardboard or paint a white piece of poster board and attach it to the cardboard.

27

Lights, Camera, . . .

To light your set, a couple of desk lamps or the overhead lights should do the trick. Don't place your set near a window or shoot outside unless it is an overcast day. Changes in lighting will cause flickering in your movie.

Experiment with the placement of the lamps. Take test shots to see how it looks.

Flat, even light is created when two lamps are placed an equal distance apart. There are little or no shadows.

Place your figure skater at center stage. Create a spotlight by directing one light onto the set.

Claymation does not require a video camera. A digital camera, smartphone camera, or tablet camera will work. Think about the camera angles you want to use while shooting your film. The angle and distance from which you capture your scene can bring your movie to life.

In a straight-on shot, the camera is lined up directly with the puppet.

Shooting the movie from above makes the puppet appear small.

A closeup shot taken from a low angle can create a dramatic effect.

. . . . Action!
Making Your Movie

It's time to make your Claymation movie! You have your storyboard, your puppet(s), your set, lights, and camera. Position the puppets on the set when you are ready to begin. Using your storyboard as a guide, start taking photos. Make sure you move your puppets in very tiny increments. The smaller the movements, the smoother the film will be. Be careful not to move the camera while taking a sequence of shots.

You can use a camera on a tripod and import your stills later into an animation program. Or you can use your smartphone or tablet camera to capture photos directly in a stop-motion animation app.

Make sure your hands are out of the frame after moving the puppet before taking the next shot.

It takes a lot of patience to make a Claymation film. Slowly move your puppet toward an object on your set to make it appear as if the puppet is moving on its own. If the puppet moves too far in each shot it will appear to jump rather than move in one fluid motion.

Now it's time to finish your movie. **Postproduction** is the last step in creating your Claymation film. Within your app or animation program you can edit your frames, removing any that don't work. This is also the time to add music or sound effects. Music can set the mood of the film. Different types of music can sound happy, sad, or suspenseful. There are all kinds of free sound effects on the Internet, or you can record your own. Adding effects to your movie will bring the action to life.

Finally, it's showtime! Stage a screening to share your sports adventure with an audience. At the end, take a bow!

If there is a scene that doesn't work, cut it!

Use clay letters to make credits for your movie. Include a title and end credits, listing yourself and anyone else who helped.

GLOSSARY

animation In film, creating the illusion of movement using still images played in a rapid sequence.

armature A wire frame that acts as a skeleton for a sculpture made with modeling clay.

frame An individual picture in a series of images.

postproduction The final stages of finishing a movie after it has been recorded that usually involves editing and adding sound.

stop-motion An animation technique that uses a series of shots showing small movements to make characters or objects appear to move.

storyboard A series of pictures that show the scenes in an animation.

FOR MORE INFORMATION

FURTHER READING

Cassidy, John, and Nicholas Berger. *The Klutz Book of Animation*. Palo Alto, CA: Klutz, 2010.

Grabham, Tim. *Movie Maker: The Ultimate Guide to Making Films*. Somerville, MA: Candlewick, 2010.

Piercy, Helen. *Animation Studio*. Somerville, MA: Candlewick, 2013.

WEBSITES

For web resources related to the subject of this book, go to: www.windmillbooks.com/weblinks and select this book's title.

INDEX